Waiting for the Forty First Day!

40 Devotions for the Season of Lent

John M. Scholte

With

Germaine Griffiths

2020
8 – 3/4
15 – 3/11
22 – 3/18
29 – 3/25
36 – 4/1
40 – 4/5 PALM SUNDAY

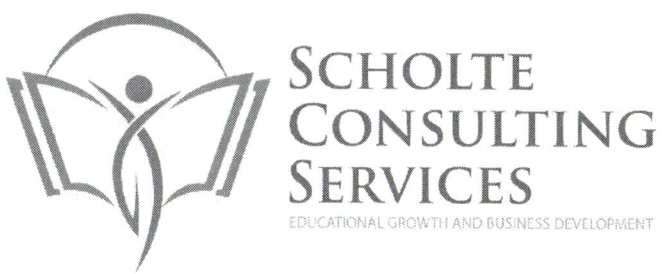

Most religions set aside certain times, or seasons of the year, for their followers to experience a deeper spirituality. The Christian religion is no different, giving its followers several opportunities to reflect upon their relationship with God and each other.

One particular time for Christians is called the Season of Lent. The Lenten Season has traditionally been a 40 day period of time between Ash Wednesday and Easter Sunday. The forty day time period comes from the story of Jesus, who prior to the start of his ministry took forty days and withdrew into the desert where he prayed, fasted, and had the self-disciple to overcome temptation.

Today, Christians take this time to pray, fast, and reflect upon their relationship with Jesus. They also repent from anything that this contemplation might reveal is hindering them from faithfully following his teachings. Like Jesus who was preparing for his coming ministry, this period is a time for Christians to prepare themselves for the coming of Easter.

Often, Lent is known for different acts of spiritual self-discipline, particularly fasting or the giving up of something one might normally enjoy. The idea is not self-punishment but to free one from some normal activity and replace it for a period of time with a deeper spiritual one.

It is our desire, that this Lenten Devotional might be one way to let go of your normal activity and take up a new spiritual discipline. An opportunity for you to reflect, renew or even begin your relationship with Jesus Christ.

Each day, starting with Ash Wednesday, we have selected a special scripture verse and written both a short Lenten devotional and prayer just for you.

Choose a time now, as you hold this devotional in your hands, whether morning, noon or evening, to read and reflect each day. We hope that through the daily use of this devotional you will grow deeper in your spiritual life and make your Easter Celebration more meaningful!

- John M. Scholte
    and
        Germaine Griffiths

Job 42:6

"Therefore I retract,
And I repent in dust and ashes."

Isaiah 61:3

"To grant those who mourn in Zion,
Giving them a garland instead of ashes,
The oil of gladness instead of
    mourning,
The mantle of praise instead of a spirit
    of fainting.
So they will be called oaks of
    righteousness,
The planting of the Lord, that He may
    be glorified."

Prayer

Dear Lord Jesus,
I know I am a sinner, and I ask for your forgiveness. I believe you died for my sins and rose from the dead. I trust and follow you as my Lord and Savior. Guide my life and help me to do your will.
In your name, amen.

Ash Wednesday

Back in the day a sign of repentance was to throw some ash upon your head. The ash represented ruin, desolation and true sorrow in ancient times.

Job practiced this ritual to show his true repentance to God for some of the disrespectful things he had said.

It's interesting to note that today many Christian Churches begin the Season of Lent by placing ash on the forehead of believers. This not only symbolizes sorrow for the things we have done but recognizes that a true relationship with God must begin with repentance.

As you begin this devotional series take some time now to pause and reflect upon your life. Do you want to begin a relationship with God? Then you must repent of your sins and ask God's forgiveness in Christ. Perhaps you already have a relationship with God. Now is the time to clear the air!

Isaiah reminds us that when we repent, our life will be filled with gladness, praise, and righteousness. And a life filled with these positive traits will glorify God.

Psalm 91:10, 12

"As for the days of our life, they
    Contain seventy years,
Or if due to strength, eighty years,
Yet their pride is but labor and
    Sorrow;
For soon it is gone and we fly away."

"So teach us to number our days,
That we may present to you a heart
    of wisdom."

Prayer

Heavenly Father, Your gifts abound and are evidenced in the dawn of every new day. Help us to meet each day with renewed hope and enthusiasm. Help us to use our knowledge wisely and to reflect Your love and compassion in all that we do. We want to learn from the past, be present with You today, and be ever mindful of the eternal glory that is our future. Help us to discern the voice of the Holy Spirit and to respond as He works in our hearts to conform us to the image of Christ, today and each tomorrow.

Lent Devotional Second Day

In the wonderful musical, *Fiddler On The Roof*, Tevye and his wife Golde sing *Sunrise, Sunset* a beautiful song with its refrain reminding us that "swiftly fly the years!" The Psalmist teaches us the same; life is swift and before you know it, "it is gone and we fly away."

As the Psalmist says we may have seventy or eighty years, and with modern healthcare maybe a bit more…so what are we doing with the time we have been given? We don't always think about this because we get so caught up in our daily activity that we lose track of time. Have you ever looked at your watch and said, "Where has the time gone?"

The Psalmist askes of us to "number our days," or in other words, pause and pay attention to the lifetime we have been given. Today, take a moment to think about your life and how you are investing it. Quietly reflect on your past activity, present actions, and future plans. Then ask God for the wisdom to live your life in awareness of the precious nature of each day.

Psalm 91:13, 14

"Do return, O Lord, how long will it
    be?
And be sorry for Your servants."

"O satisfy us in the morning with Your
    lovingkindness,
That we may sing for joy and be glad
    all our days."

Prayer

Lord, You alone know what is truly in our hearts and minds, and You alone know the depth of the struggles we face. Our inner conflicts evoke strong emotions and the intensity of our feelings can overwhelm us. When this happens we need only to open our Bibles and turn to the wisdom of Scripture for help. We are grateful that we can come to You, Lord, with any personal struggle and not only will you listen, but if we are patient and obedient, You will guide us into resolution and peace. We are thankful for Your presence and Your promises. We are blessed by your steadfast love and faithfulness.

Lent Devotional Third Day

One characteristic of my family is that we often have animated discussions at family gatherings. Not personally attacking each other, but a serious wrestling with each other's ideas. All done in love of course, but often to those outside the family they may appear conflictual. However it is in this loving struggle that I have grown the most. I am happy to say because of this process my ideas and understanding have matured.

Common within many Psalms in the Bible is a serious wrestling and struggle between the Psalmist and God. "How long will it be?" asked the Psalmist in the anguish of relief not yet granted and with a surprising boldness of impatience with God. When will the Psalmist be satisfied? Only with the coming of the Messiah!

Lent is a time when you can wrestle and struggle with God over the issues of your life you may not understand. Don't be afraid, be as bold as the Psalmist. Take time now to share your concerns. Your answer will come in the life, death, and resurrection of Jesus!

John 12:32, 35, 36

"And I, if I am lifted up from the earth, will draw all men to Myself."

"So Jesus said to them, "For a little while longer the Light is among you, Walk while you have the Light, so that darkness will not overtake you; he who walks in the darkness does not know where he goes.""

"While you have the Light, believe in the Light, so that you may become sons of Light."

Prayer

Gracious Father, we are blessed to be able to bask in the light of Your love and truth. We pray that you will give us the strength and courage to resist the temptation of sin and the desire to hide our disobedience from You. Help us to be open and honest in our confessions, exposing even the darkest of secrets in our hearts to the light of Your grace and forgiveness. Help us to always run toward the light and away from the darkness.

Lent Devotional Fourth Day

To define the subject of a painting through the use of light and darkness is called Chiaroscuro. A technique that became one of the features of the Baroque Era of art and can be seen best in Rembrandt, the era's greatest master.

Rembrandt was well versed in the Bible's metaphor of light and darkness and created his works with that in mind. For him the darkness stood as a place for his subjects to hide their naturally sinful life from the searching and penetrating light of God's truth. The character of his subjects was defined through the use of Chiaroscuro.

The Bible defines life and people in the same way. Jesus, who is the Light, calls us out of the darkness to have a relationship with him. From this relationship we become the people of light. Our character is no longer defined by darkness. "For a little while longer" you have an opportunity to live a life defined by light and not darkness. Today, give up those things hidden in darkness and step out into a renewed life defined by the Light.

Psalm 17: 5, 8, 9, 11, 15

"My steps have held fast to Your
   Paths.
My feet have not slipped."

"Keep me as the apple of the eye;
Hide me in the shadow of Your wings"

"From the wicked who despoil me;
My deadly enemies who surround me."

"They have now surrounded us in our steps;
They set their eyes to cast us down to the ground."

"As for me, I shall behold Your face in righteousness;
I will be satisfied with your likeness
   When I awake."

Prayer

Father, help us to discern Your voice and Your truth above the noise of the world. Help us to guard against distractions that would threaten our commitment to You. We desire to listen to You with an open and humble heart and ask for Your wisdom to guide our choices.

Lent Devotional Fifth Day

Not too long ago I saw a YouTube video of a baby, born almost totally blind, seeing his parents for the first time. After he was fitted with special lenses, his parents called out to him. As soon as their eyes met the baby broke into a wonderful smile. He looked back and forth at both his parents with such joy. His parents were calling his name and I could tell, through the sound of their voices, he was the apple of their eye.

The palmist wants to remain as the apple of God's eye, but he is afraid he will lose this cherished spot because he is surrounded by negative people who are trying to pull him down. However, he knows keeping his focus on God through the special lens of righteousness will bring him the joy and comfort he desires.

Do you feel, like the Psalmist, surrounded by negative people trying to bring you down? Focus your mind's eye on the special lens of Jesus, who is the very evidence that You are the apple of God's eye, the one he loves, and protects.

II Peter 2: 18-20

"For they mouth empty, boastful words and, by appealing to the lustful desires of the flesh, they entice people who are just escaping from those who live in error."

"They promise them freedom, while they themselves are slaves of depravity—for "people are slaves to whatever has mastered them.""

"If they have escaped the corruption of the world by knowing our Lord and Savior Jesus Christ and are again entangled in it and are overcome, they are worse off at the end than they were at the beginning."

Prayer

Lord, we pray to be ever mindful that we represent the believer's values to the world. Help us never to betray or minimize the truth of Your Word. Help us to be bold in our convictions and to speak and act in a manner that honors Christ, reflects His love, and exemplifies the wisdom of the Holy Spirit who guides us.

Lent Devotional Sixth Day 3/2/2020

The Apostle Peter was writing to Christians that had teachers who knew and were well versed in the faith, but chose to teach and live a lifestyle of sin. Apparently, these teachers even tried through their teachings to entice others to live the same sinful lifestyle.

Peter warned those encountering these teachers, particularly young Christians, to not become entangled in this kind of hypocrisy. He teaches that it would be better for a person to never have known the truth than to have known it and then turn away to a life of sin.

The reason is simple; a life of hypocrisy does the most damage to a Christian witness. Not only for the Christian hypocrite, but for Christianity as a whole. The consequences for sin are universal, but it is worse for the Christian because they represent the truth to all.

I am sure you have heard the saying "talk the talk, walk the walk." Take a moment now to review your witness. Ask yourself, "Am I consistent with Jesus' teachings both in what I say and do?"

Prayers for: Larry & Kathy
Shelley & Sam & Ruth
Corona Virus Patients

Luke 21: 34

"Be on your guard, so that your hearts will not be weighted down with dissipation and drunkenness and the worries of life, and that day will not come on you suddenly like a trap."

Prayer

Heavenly Father, we pray that we never forget where we are going and how we are to get there. Heaven is our ultimate destination and Your Word is our roadmap. Help us to travel the righteous path and to keep our eyes on the promise of our future home with You. We know there will be bumps in the road, detours, accidents, and delays on our journey through this life. Help us to remember that any hardship we face here cannot compare with the glory that will be ours one day. On that day, reconciled with You, we will celebrate the joy of our new bodies and let go of the old. Eternity with You is the promise that makes life worth living and death just the beginning.

Lent Devotional Seventh Day 3/3/2020

    A personal self-defense coach will tell you to always "be on your guard." When you complete your shopping don't look like you are wondering around looking for your car. Don't fumble through your purse looking for your keys. Keep your keys out and ready to use, look around you and be aware of your surroundings. Walk as if you are sure of your destination. These and other tips will make you less of a target for a possible mugging.

    Jesus reminds us that we must also be on our guard with our hearts so that we are not robbed of the joyful celebration when he returns. People can be "weighted down" and miss out because they are not attentive to their spiritual life. Their focus is on the party scene or they are busy creating relational drama in their lives, and missing the true joy of living God's plan for them.

    Lent is an opportunity to "be on your guard!" Today ask yourself, "Have I been living the party scene?" "Do I create relational drama?" If so, give that up for Lent and focus your heart on Jesus and living your life for him.

Psalm 27: 13, 14

"I would have despaired unless I had
   Believed that I would see the
   Goodness of the Lord;
In the land of the living."

"Wait for the Lord;
Be strong and let your heart take
   Courage;
Yes, wait for the Lord."

Prayer

Lord, You are our help and our shield. If we trust in Your holy name You will have mercy upon us. You will deliver us from sorrow and save us from trouble. Only You can truly see what is in the heart and mind, and only You can ease the pain and suffering that lives there. Give us the courage to place our confidence in the truth of Your Word and in Your everlasting love. If we seek You, we 'shall not lack for any good thing.' We will find our strength, our purpose, and our path of righteousness in You.

Lent Devotional Eighth Day

If you search the internet for the top ten traits of successful people, many, if not all, will have the trait of self-confidence on the list. There is no doubt that successful people succeed, overcome obstacles, and bust through barriers because they believe in their abilities to meet the challenge.

The Palmist, King David, shows the trait of confidence in a different light. Although a very successful king, when he wrote this Psalm, his troubles were crushing the life out of him. <u>He didn't have the answers or the ability to solve his problems, but he knew who did.</u> He would have despaired if it wasn't for his confidence in "the goodness of the Lord; in the land of the living." He placed his confidence in God who would give him a practical answer for his current problems.

Are you feeling crushed by your current problems and challenges? You may even be a pretty self-confident person, but at present you feel close to despair. Today, and throughout Lent, place your confidence in God. Trust that he will provide a solution. Be strong and let your heart take courage!

Philippians 3: 17 - 20

"Brethren, join in following my example, and observe those who walk according to the pattern you have in us.

For many walk, of whom I often told you, and now tell you even weeping, that they are enemies of the cross of Christ,

Whose end is destruction, whose god is their appetite, and whose glory is in their shame, who set their minds on earthly things.

For our citizenship is in heaven, from which also we eagerly wait for a Savior, the Lord Jesus Christ."

Prayer

Father, we pray to be ever mindful that the ways of the world are ready and eager to tempt us, stumble us, and draw us away from our faith. Help us to stand strong in our convictions and live a life that is consistent with the wisdom of Your Word. <u>Place true believers in our paths to support and encourage us</u> and to keep us accountable for our choices.

Prayer for: Sylvia Hoskins
Kathy + Larry
Sam + Ruth for Shelley
Katey

3/5/2020

Lent Devotional Ninth Day

Maybe you have heard, as I have in different conversations, someone say that the world seems to be getting more and more sinful all the time. And it may seem like that perception would be correct. Social media has been a forum for posting the worst of ourselves as a way to achieve celebrity. Reality television has placed conflict and relational drama on a pedestal for the world to see. What was once the subculture of our society has now been declared the norm.

However, when you read Philippians it is evident that society hasn't changed that much. In the Apostle Paul's day peoples actions and thoughts were just as twisted and shameful as they are today. Like today, the debased things were being glorified.

Another thing that hasn't changed since Paul's day is that Christian are to be examples of a different pattern of living. We walk, eagerly waiting for a Savior, members of a heavenly society, whose actions and thoughts glorify Christ. Reflect today on what people observe in your life. Will they see a different pattern of living in you?

Be not discouraged! We are members of a heavenly society. Show it in the way we live. Seek support of other faithful followers.

Psalm 118: 26

"Blessed is the one who comes in the
 name of the Lord;
We have blessed you from the house
 Of the Lord."

Matthew 23: 39

"For I say to you, from now on you will not see me until you say, 'Blessed is he who comes in the name of the Lord!'"

Prayer

Heavenly Father, we thank You for showing us the way: If the faithful seek truth they will find it in the life, ministry, death, and resurrection of Your Son, Jesus Christ. If the sinner asks for forgiveness, he will find redemption at the foot of the cross. And if the believer humbly receives the gift of salvation, he will live in Your Presence forever. Please help us to be worthy of Your great love and the ultimate sacrifice You made for us in the name of that great love. All glory and praise is Yours.

Lent Devotional Tenth Day

When Jesus quoted the blessing of Psalm 118 he was standing on the Mount of Olives looking across the Kidron Valley at a panorama of Jerusalem. It wouldn't be long and the crowd from the city would be embracing him as the coming King with palm branches. But their blessings would turn to curses only a few days later. The reason is the crowd's words were not authentic. They were only spoken in the energy of the moment, they clearly did not see him as the blessed one for whom those words were meant.

Unlike the crowd, Jesus knew that when he crossed the valley the real work of redemption would begin. Only through this work, being his death and resurrection, would people really see him as the Christ and authentically say the Psalmist's blessing.

The same is true for you today. It is impossible for you to see Jesus as Savior, until you have confessed your faith in his redemptive work. First confess authentically, then say faithfully, "Blessed is the one who comes in the name of the Lord."

Exodus 33: 4, 5, 6

"When the people heard this sad word, they went into morning, and none of them put on his ornaments.

For the Lord had said to Moses, "Say to the sons of Israel, 'You are an obstinate people; should I go up in your midst for one moment, I would destroy you. Now therefore, put off your ornaments from you, that I may know what I shall do with you.'

So the sons of Israel stripped themselves of their ornaments, from Mount Horeb onward."

Prayer

Lord, You know us better than we know ourselves. You know how much we struggle with pride and vanity. Help us to be open to Your direction and Your will for us. Shape us into believers who cooperate with and yield to the guidance of the Holy Spirit—not willful beings who resist Your design for our lives.

Lent Devotional Eleventh Day

The dictionary defines "obstinate" as stubbornly refusing to change one's opinion or chosen course of action, despite attempts to persuade one to do so. Synonyms for the word include: stubborn, unyielding, inflexible, and unbending.

The Hebrews coming out of Egypt fit this definition well. Despite everything that God had done, sending a deliverer from bondage, they remained stubborn, unyielding, inflexible, and unbending. Like the days of Noah, God wanted to start anew. When the Hebrews heard God's anger with their haughty attitudes they mourned and removed their jewelry. The jewelry came from the same stash used to build a golden calf, the ultimate example of their obstinance. The point is God needed pliable people to accomplish his plan.

Today God's plans still cannot be accomplished through obstinate people. While we wait for Jesus' return, we must strip away any stubborn attitude and be open to his discipleship. Are you yielding to God? Are you bending to his will for your life? Are you open to his purposes?

I Corinthians 10: 12, 13

"Therefore let him who thinks he stands take heed that he does not fall.

No temptation has overtaken you but such as is common to man; and God is faithful, who will not allow you to be tempted beyond what you are able, but with the temptation will provide the way of escape also, so that you will be able to endure it."

II Corinthians 12: 9a

"And He has said to me, 'My grace is sufficient for you, for power is perfected in weakness.'"

Prayer

Lord, help us to seek You first when we are tempted to turn from righteousness. Bless us with self-restraint. Deliver us from the behaviors we know will hurt You and the people we love. Help us to accept the trials that we endure, knowing that Your ultimate purpose is to grow our character and bring us closer to You. When we cannot understand, let us trust.

Lent Devotional Twelfth Day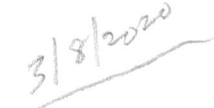

I Cor. 10: 13 is one of the most miss-quoted passages in the Bible. People confuse tough times that storm into our lives with temptations that draw us away from Christ. However, in both situations I hear people say, "God will never give you more than you can handle." Well, this is only true with temptation, but God is still faithful in both situations.

First, <u>temptation</u>. These are enticements to sin by Satan in a deliberate attempt to bring out our worst, to bind us. God is faithful to "<u>provide a way of escape</u>." Here God will never give us more than we can handle.

Second, <u>trials and tribulations</u>. Difficult events that inevitably come to every life, as a result of living in a fallen world. Honestly, many are <u>more than we can handle</u>: the loss of a loved one, cancer, the ravages of war. However, God is still faithful because His sufficient grace gives us the power to continue living even with the most unbearable circumstances.

Today, in whatever circumstance you find yourself, know that God is faithful!

Luke 13: 23, 24

"And someone said to Him, 'Lord, are there just a few who are being saved?' And He said to them,

'Strive to enter through the narrow door; for many, I tell you, will seek to enter and will not be able.'"

Prayer

Father, you have given us one lifetime to make the most important decision we will ever make. Help us to commit to the truth of salvation as the Bible teaches. Jesus is the way, the truth, and the life. He is our Shepherd. It is His voice we listen for and it is His Word that we follow. Christ alone can save us and only He can promise everlasting life. The world offers up other prophets to us, such as Buddha and Mohammad. But they were just men. They could not save themselves, much less the world. Thank you for the precious gift of Your Son and the promise of His eternal love for those who would believe. We pray to be worthy of His sacrifice.

Lent Devotional Thirteenth Day

Today there is a common idea circulating through our society, even among some Christians, that there are many different ways to heaven. This idea is commonly called "Universalism" by theologians.

Although this concept is complex and there are many intricacies related to its philosophy, one simple illustration captures its most basic teachings. You are standing in a room which has many doors, you can open and pass through any door you choose because they all lead to heaven.

Jesus teaches otherwise, he said there are only two doors. One wide door, that leads to death and destruction and one narrow door that leads to eternal life. For a person to be saved they must strive to enter through the narrow door, however there is one catch to taking this door. It will not remain unlocked indefinitely.

Lent is the time to be honest with ourselves about this truth, even if society thinks differently; there is only one door to salvation and it is narrowed by time. Seek to open the door before it is too late.

Psalm 63: 1, 6, 8

"O God, You are my God; I seek
    You earnestly;
My soul thirsts for You, my flesh
    Yearns for You,
In a dry and weary land where there
    Is no water."

"When I remember You on my bed,
I meditate on You in the night
    Watches,"

"My soul clings to you;
Your right hand upholds me."

Prayer

Heavenly Father, help us to be passionate in our love for You. When we feel discouraged or experience an emptiness and a longing in our souls, let us remember that You alone were meant to fill us up. Happiness is fleeting, but a joy that is lasting comes from loving You. Nothing else can truly satisfy or sustain the yearnings of the human heart.

Lent Devotional Fourteenth Day

One of my most favorite quotes comes from the English writer and Christian apologist, G.K. Chesterton, who once wrote, "Let your religion be less of a theory and more of a love affair." I think this captures the feeling of the Psalmist. His passionate love for God comes through with this psalm which would later be used in the early church for daily public prayers.

When you really love someone, you experience the same feelings the Psalmist expressed. It could be a spouse, parent, child, or good friend. When you love someone, you intentionally seek them out to spend time with them. When they are not with you, you look forward to their return. They are constantly on your mind. You think about your conversations and activities. Being with them refreshes your spirits and gives you a sense of encouragement.

I can see why the early church used this psalm in daily public prayers. We should be reminded daily that we need to have, like the Psalmist, more of a love affair with God in our daily lives.

Daniel 12: 2, 3, 4

"Many of those who sleep in the dust of the ground will awake, these to everlasting life, but others to disgrace and everlasting contempt.

Those who have insight will shine brightly like the brightness of the expanse of heaven, and those who lead the many to righteousness, like the stars forever and ever.

But as for you, Daniel, conceal these words and seal up the book until the end of time; many will go back and forth, and knowledge will increase."

Prayer

Father, we are blessed by Your hand on our lives. We are inspired to persevere in our spiritual walk because You give us hope. It is a hope that transcends our humanity and the destruction and suffering that touches each of our lives in this world. It is the promise of eternal life in Your presence that gives us the confidence to rise above despair.

Lent Devotional Fifteenth Day

There was a study done after the holocaust on why certain people survived and others died even with equal health and social position when they arrived at the concentration camps. The conclusion found that those who retained hope had the best possibility of survival. The Apostle Paul said that three essential elements were needed for humankind to survive: Faith, Hope and Love.

Most of the Book of Daniel is consumed with the apocalyptic suffering that God's people would experience at the end of the age. However, in the last chapter an angel comes to Daniel and gives him a message of hope. Something God's people could hang on too in the mists of despair. The message was of victory over death, and the vindication of those living Godly lives under torment.

It is a proven fact that there is no way to deal with disparages in life without hope. This is why God has given us a new hope in Jesus whose resurrection gives us the promise that all things will work together for our good even in tough times.

Luke 6: 43, 44

"For there is no good tree which produces bad fruit, nor, on the other hand, a bad tree which produces good fruit.

For each tree is known by its own fruit. For men do not gather figs from thorns, nor do they pick grapes from a briar bush."

Prayer

Gracious Heavenly Father, we pray to be the best disciples we can be. We desire to study and learn Your Word, and pass along Your teachings to others. As we follow You, Lord, imprint Your message of love and forgiveness on our hearts. Bring to remembrance Your laws and show us how to live out our lives according to Scripture. We strive to incorporate Your teachings in every area of our lives, exemplifying our devotion to You and our trust in the power of Your message. Help us overcome the obstacles to our obedience so that we may be seen as successful in Your eyes.

Lent Devotional Sixteenth Day

There are many spiritual teachers available to us today. Including the Dalai Lama, Deepak Chopra, Paulo Coelho, Thich Nhat Hanh, Sri Sri Ravi Shankar, and Rhonda Byrne. All these people's teachings are best sellers! Many people follow them.

In Jesus' day, there were also many spiritual teachers that people could follow. So on a hillside in Galilee Jesus laid out the basics of his teachings in a sermon called The Beatitudes. Then He said something that may appear strange at first glance. He talks about two different types of trees, the fruit they produce, and how fruit from one type of tree cannot be found on another type.

Jesus wanted people to decide which teacher they were going to follow. His teachings, the best fruit, or another that produces bad fruit. Jesus wanted a commitment to follow Him completely, and no one else.

Are you willing to make Jesus your teacher completely? To be his disciple? To turn every area of your life- mental, physical, social and spiritual- over to him?

Psalm 39: 4, 5, 6

"Lord, make me to know my end
And what is the extent of my days;
Let me know how transient I am.

Behold, you have made my days as
    Handbreadths,
And my lifetime as nothing in Your
    Sight;
Surely every man at his best is a
    mere breath.

Surely every man walks about as a
    Phantom;
Surely they make an uproar for
    Nothing;
He amasses riches and does not know
    Who will gather them."

Prayer

Father, help us to see the beauty and value of each day through Your eyes. In all of our thoughts and deeds, help us to discern foolishness from wisdom. To never forget to renew our commitment to You with every sunrise and to declare our gratitude for Your goodness with every sunset.

Lent Devotional Seventeenth Day

Several years ago I was working for a retirement community when one of the residents celebrated his 100 birthday. At the party we sat and talked together about his life and all the things that had taken place during his lifetime. He told me that when he was younger he thought 100 years was a long time, but now that he had lived them, it seemed like only the blink of an eye. Psalm 39 confirms his feelings.

Think about how the Psalmist writes about a lifespan. It is transient, a handbreadth, nothing in God's sight, at best a mere breath, only a phantom. And notice what the Psalmist says about what people spend this time on. Making an uproar for nothing, amassing things with no purpose.

This Psalm is really a prayer for awareness of the brevity of life and to respect the fact that life goes by fast. What are you going to do in the blink of an eye?

Well, you have two choices. You can live in an uproar, figuring, "Eat, drink, and be merry, for tomorrow we die." Or, you can live for the Lord, the only option which gives life an eternal purpose.

Romans 2: 14, 15, 16

"For when Gentiles who do not have the Law do instinctively the things of the law, these, not having the law, are a law to themselves,

In that way they show the work of the Law written in their hearts, their conscience bearing witness and their thoughts alternately accusing them or else defending them,

On the day when, according to my gospel, God will judge the secrets of men through Christ Jesus."

Prayer

Loving Father, thank you for the indwelling of the Holy Spirit in the heart and mind of a believer. It is the Holy Spirit that guides us, encourages us, convicts us, and corrects us. Help us to recognize His voice and respond to His loving discipline. We are grateful Lord, for without the Holy Spirit we could not, in any measure, be conformed to the image of Christ.

Lent Devotional Eighteenth Day

It has been said that if intuition is a person's sixth sense then conscience is the seventh sense. The majority of people are born with this "seventh sense," an inner feeling or voice that acts alongside our thoughts as a guide to the rightness or wrongness of one's behavior. Only about 4% of the population are thought not to have one, and they are categorized as sociopaths.

Barring a mental disorder, the greater majority of people have a conscience and the Apostle Paul points out that it can be as effective at convicting or acquitting people of sin as the Law of Moses.

Today we live in a society where many people are living their lives as experts in suppressing their conscience. But Paul reminds us to tune our conscience through the gospel of Christ Jesus. This "seventh sense" can assist us to live righteously, with no fear that God knows the secrets of our inner thoughts, because our behavior and thoughts are guided by a conscience that is open to the gospel.

Numbers 13: 25, 26, 27

"When they returned from spying out the land, at the end of forty days.

They proceeded to come to Moses and Aaron and to all the congregation of the sons of Israel in the wilderness of Paran, at Kadesh; and they brought back word to them and to all the congregation and showed them the fruit of the Land.

Thus they told him, and said, 'We went in to the land where you sent us; and it certainly does flow with milk and honey, and this is its fruit.'"

Prayer

Lord, the world offers us immediate gratification. But Scripture tells us that it is the very act of waiting that develops patience and teaches us perseverance. Help us to set aside the urgency of the world and reflect on Your constancy, Your long-suffering, and Your welcoming love. We wait eagerly for Your return, Jesus. In the meantime, help us to embrace the virtue of patience as we grow in faith.

Lent Devotional Nineteenth Day

The neo soul/indie pop band Fritz and The Tantrums recorded the song, "Out Of My League." The lyrics are about a guy waiting 40 days and 40 nights to be with a girl. The problem? She is really out of his league. But it's worth the wait when she becomes his girlfriend. The number 40 has been a sign of waiting, preparation, testing, and even judgement since biblical times.

In the time of Moses, after the Hebrews escaped Egypt, they came to the Promised Land and sent spies who investigated the area for 40 days. When they reported back, the spies gave such an overwhelming report that the Israelites refused to trust God and take the land. Israel's punishment for this lack of faith was 40 years of wandering in the desert.

The Lenten Season lasts for 40 days and is a time of waiting for Jesus, in whose league we don't really belong. Here's the real overwhelming report; He wants to be with us anyway. You need to totally trust that he is your Savior and really does want a personal relationship with you. If you do, you won't wander in a spiritual desert.

Psalm 32: 1, 3, 4, 5

"How blessed is he whose
   transgression is forgiven,
Whose sin is covered!

When I kept silent about my sin, my
   body wasted away
Through my groaning all day long.

For day and night Your hand was
   heavy upon me;
My vitality was drained away as
   with the fever heat of summer.

I acknowledge my sin to You,
And my iniquity I did not hide;
I said, 'I will confess my
   transgressions to the Lord;'
And You forgave the guilt of my sin."

Prayer

Father, our hearts are sickened with guilt, regret, shame, and self-loathing. It can be debilitating. Mercifully, You will hear our confessions and release us with Your forgiveness. Your love cleanses us, lifts our sickness, and allows us to move forward.

Lent Devotional Twentieth Day

At the end of his life, Johnny Cash performed a cover of the song "Hurt," by Nine Inch Nails, along with a music video. Both became very successful. I think part of the success was in the connection he made between sinful living and physical bodily pain and depletion. The mournful lyrics acknowledge what we often do to ourselves when our lives are filled with guilt and regret.

The Psalmist makes the same connection. Sin affects us emotionally and physically. With sin the possibilities are greater that our bodies will waste away, and our vitality will drain away if we don't deal with the sin in our lives.

Some Christians have claimed, on the basis of texts like this one that all human disease comes as a result of sin. But this is not what Scripture is teaching here. Scripture is teaching that the guilt of sin can weigh so heavy upon us that it can make us sick. However, there is a cure; confess and acknowledge our sins and God is faithful and just and will forgive us our sins and purify us from all unrighteousness.

II Corinthians 5: 14, 15

"For the love of Christ controls us, having concluded this, that one died for all, therefore all died;

And He died for all, so that they who live might no longer live for themselves, but for Him who died and rose on their behalf."

Prayer

Father, You are our creator. All life originates and is sustained by You. There can be no other starting point for those of us who love You. Help us to make Your Word the "fixed point" from which we navigate the challenges of this world and from which we find the answers to life's questions. We can stand strong in any storm if You are with us and we are obedient to Your Word. Our faith secures us and gives us confidence because it is built on a foundation of truth and the laws of God. Love is at our core.

Lent Devotional Twenty First Day

I begin my Introduction to Ethics course asking my students, "What is your core ethic?" Can they state in a succinct way what controls, motivates or drives their actions? Of course everyone has a core ethic, but many students are unable to state one. The majority of students have never given it much thought, which may be the case with most people. To me it's a bit frightening that some people could be living with no self-awareness of what is motivating their behaviors.

Paul has no doubt what the core ethic is for Christians. He states very succinctly, "For the love of Christ controls us." He teaches that Christ's life, death and resurrection can captured the Christians hearts so completely that Christ's love becomes the ultimate ethic to a Christian's life.

What is your core ethic? What motivates you? What is the basis for the decisions you make? Take some time today to meditate on these questions. Ask yourself how your answers might reflect your life in Christ.

Luke 15: 3, 4, 5, 6, 7

"So He told them this parable, saying

'What man among you, if he has a hundred sheep and has lost one of them, does not leave the ninety-nine in the open pasture and go after the one which is lost until he finds it?

When he has found it, he lays it on his shoulders, rejoining.

And when he comes home, he calls together his friends and his neighbors, saying to them, 'Rejoice with me, for I have found my sheep which was lost!'

I tell you that in the same way, there will be more joy in heaven over one sinner who repents than over ninety-nine righteous persons who need no repentance.'"

Prayer

Loving Father, thank you for valuing us as individuals, pursuing us for Your kingdom. Your love for us is constant and patient. How blessed are we that when we stray, You welcome us back with open arms.

Lent Devotional Twenty Second Day

Christianity is unique because, of all religions of the world, the faith of Christianity sends no person on a journey or search for God. Quite the opposite, it sends God on a journey or search for humankind. Martin Luther, the protestant reformer, referred to God as the "Hound of Heaven." God pursues us like a hound pursues a fox through meadows and woodlands, never giving up the hunt.

Martin Luther's idea captures the point of this parable; how valuable and significant we are to God. He will never stop searching for us until he finds us, and when he does he will never let us go. The parable appears in the center of Luke's Gospel, and is also its central point. Luke is showing us how much people matter to God!

The last part of the parable speaks of sin, repentance and joy and reminds me of an old hymn. "Amazing Grace! How sweet the sound that saved a wretch like me! I once was lost, but now am found; was blind, but now I see."

Psalm 53: 1, 6

"The fool has said in his heart, 'There
   Is no God,'
They are corrupt, and have committed
   Abominable injustice;
There is no one who does good.

Oh, that the salvation of Israel
   Would come out of Zion!"

Prayer

Father, help us to discern foolishness from wisdom in the small and the big things in life. The fool denies God's existence and rejects Jesus Christ and His plan for our salvation. The fool relies on his own understanding and seeks to please himself, desiring the approval of the world. Wisdom comes from studying Your Word and applying it to our lives. Wisdom is choosing to love You above all others, asking for Your forgiveness, and living out our lives according to Your will. Help us to be ever mindful that foolishness leads to separation and death, but wisdom brings eternal life.

Lent Devotional Twenty Third Day

There is an old question that comes out of wisdom literature, "Is it possible to take from the fools and add to the wise?" As a Professors, I ask myself this question every time I begin teaching a new class. I suppose I believe it is possible, otherwise why would I continue to teach? However, to bring wisdom to a fool is not an easy task, and to this, the Psalmist would agree.

The Psalmist defines a fool as someone who thinks they are impervious to accountability believing that no judgement should be made on their actions. And since there is no one who is righteous enough to teach them wisdom, the fool remains the fool. The fool's Salvation come from Zion.

In the Bible, Zion represents the place where God resides. We would call it heaven. From heaven comes the Wisdom of God, the righteous one, the salvation of fools, who is able to judge and transform foolish hearts. Christ's life, death and resurrection gives us the answer, "Yes, it is possible to take from the fools and add to the wise."

Revelation 19: 9, 10

"Then he said to me, 'Write, Blessed are those who are invited to the marriage supper of the Lamb.' And he said to me, 'These are true words of God.'

Then I fell at his feet to worship him. But he said to me, 'Do not do that; I am a fellow servant of yours and your brethren who hold the testimony of Jesus; worship God. For the testimony of Jesus is the spirit of prophecy.'"

Prayer

The joy we know from loving You Lord does more than sustain us and nourish our souls. Your favor helps us to press onward in our Christian lives with hope and determination. The blessings You bestow on us are faithful reminders of Your presence and Your love and Your desire to see us transformed to the image of Christ. What a gift it is to feel secure in Your steadfastness and Your goodness! Thank you for the greatest blessing of all, Your Son Jesus, and the invitation to glorify Him forever.

Lent Devotional Twenty Fourth Day

  This is one of seven "Beatitude" type sayings in the Book of Revelation. The same word "blessed" is used here as in Matthew 5. The root word in the Greek means "happy," but in the form that it appears in both settings, it means more than an emotion. It refers to a joy that surpasses understanding. It is a transcendent joy that is a sign of spiritual maturity in Christ. Unlike an emotion, that comes and goes depending upon circumstances, it is a steady sense of well-being which is constantly present in a Christian's life.

  Today we need to reflect on this level of Christian maturity. How can we have that kind of blessedness in our lives?

  First, we must have an invitation to the "marriage supper of the Lamb." This supper is the joyful eternal communion we have with Christ when he returns. The invitation comes only with faith in Christ.

  Second, follow what John was told to do, hold the testimony of Jesus within you and worship God. Be resolute, in this season, to become one of the "blessed" by following these "true words of God."

II Kings 4: 2b, 3, 4, 5, 6, 7

"And she said, 'Your maidservant has nothing in the house except a jar of oil.'

Then he said, 'Go, borrow vessels at large for yourself from all your neighbors, even empty vessels; do not get a few.

And you shall go in and shut the door behind you and your sons, and pour out into all these vessels, and you shall set aside what is full.

So she went from him and shut the door behind her and her sons; they were bringing the vessels to her and she poured.

When the vessels were full, she said to her son, 'Bring me another vessel.' And he said to her, 'There is not one vessel more.' And the oil stopped.

Then she came and told the man of God. And he said, 'Go, sell the oil and pay your debts, and you and your sons can live on the rest.'"

Prayer

Thank you Jesus for Your provision and Your protection. We rely on Your promises and trust Your power to supply all of our needs.

✓ 3/20/2020

Lent Devotional Twenty Fifth Day

There is an old saying, "God helps those who help themselves." It may be apropos to this story of the widow. Her husband had been a part of a religious community connected with the prophet Elisha. Apparently, after her husband died she had been left in debt, and the creditors were coming to collect. If she couldn't pay, her sons would become indentured servants. So she calls out to the prophet, reminding him of her husband's faithful service. Then she follows through with everything Elisha tells her to do.

You have to admire her determined character. She takes the initiative to find the solution to her problems. She doesn't know what the answer will be, but she recognizes that if she doesn't do something the answer will be nothing. In the end God provides for her to pay her debt and have additional income to meet her living expenses.

More often than not, I have found this widow's story true, if I take the intuitive God provides for my needs. I may not know how it will work out, but I can always trust God will provide. The same is true for you!

"Always trust that God will provide."

Isaiah 43: 13

"Even from eternity I am He,
And there is none who can deliver
   Out of my hand:
I act and who can reverse it?"

Prayer

Your love is constant and true, Father. No matter our wickedness and selfishness Your promise of salvation is unwavering. When we contrast the beauty of Your creation with the ugliness of mankind, we are at once in awe of Your compassion and shamed by our depraved nature. We are undeserving, yet You offer us redemption. We are immoral and yet You cleanse us with Your holiness. We are defiant and still You forgive our transgressions and comfort us with Your grace. We give You heartache and in return You give us Christ. Lord, we pray to be deserving of Your profound and steadfast love. Thank you for never giving up on us. We sing Your praises and proclaim Your goodness!

Lent Devotional Twenty Sixth Day

This is one of the great statements of Hope in Isaiah! When God saves his people nothing can change this action. He will not repeal what he has already declared and accomplished. And nothing else can accomplish what He has done.

For ancient Israel, God delivered them from their bondage in Egypt and made a covenant with them. He would be their God, their deliverer. They would be His people, and no other god would be able to change this relationship. No other god can deliver like his mighty hand. Even to the point that if they broke their covenantal promise, and they did, he would still honor his promise.

God continues to save his people from bondage today. He did it through the life, death and resurrection of His Son, Jesus. He will not repeal what he has already declared and accomplished. And nothing else can accomplish or reverse what He has done.

This is our hope, despite the times we break our promises to him, he still honors his promise in Christ to us!

Philippians 2: 25

"But I thought it necessary to send to you Epaphroditus, my brother and fellow worker and fellow soldier, who is also your messenger and minister to my need."

Prayer

Lord, we are grateful to serve You in the family of believers. We pray for unity and harmony in our community. When conflicts arise, help us to resolve them with respect and love for one another. When differences threaten to separate us, guide us to a peaceful resolution by the wisdom of Your Word. Discipline us to examine the personal motives and intentions that underlie our behaviors towards others and help us to make corrections where needed. Show us how to promote and heal relationships with honesty and humility and give us the courage to apologize and ask for forgiveness when we have wronged another. We pray to be able to accept and embrace all believers. Mold our hearts into the hearts of servants, carrying Your message boldly into all the world.

Lent Devotional Twenty Seventh Day

If you are looking for baby names, Epaphroditus is available! Great biblical reputation included with the name too. The root word of the name in Greek means "lovely," and Epaphroditus lived up to his name's meaning.

A very close friend to the Apostle Paul, he is sent as Paul's representative to the church in the city of Philippi. It seems he was a member of the church there and had brought financial support from the church to Paul in Rome. While in Rome he became gravely ill and almost died, but was able to survive and carried Paul's letter back on his return to the church. His service to Paul, and his servant attitude, endeared him to the apostle and gained him high praise.

No matter what name our parents gave us at our birth, if we are Christians, we live under the name of Christ. We are His representatives sent into the world to share His message. This is our service to Christ, and to do it well we need to have a servant attitude. An attitude that will give a lovely meaning to the Christian name.

Psalm 126: 5, 6

"Those who sow in tears shall reap
    With joyful shouting.

He who goes to and fro weeping,
    carrying his bag of seed,
Shall indeed come again with a shout
    of joy, bringing his sheaves with him."

Prayer

What a comfort it is to know that You will never forsake us, Father! Life confronts us with loss without preparing us for the depth of sadness and emptiness it brings. Repeated loss threatens to destroy us. But for God, we might languish in despair! Thank you Lord, for giving us a reason for the hope that is in us! Your faithfulness and love pull us back from desolation. The world would leave us in sorrow, but You would give us back our joy. You will bring new opportunities and blessings out of the ashes. You will help us find our way back to a purposeful life. You will temper our grief with blissful anticipation of a life beyond this one. Thank you, Jesus!

Lent Devotional Twenty Eighth Day

This may seem to be a very strange section of the Psalms. Speaking about tears and weeping while sowing and then shouts of joy at harvest. A little background on this text is helpful. If you read the books of Ezra and Nehemiah you find that Israel had been defeated by the Babylonians and driven into exile for 70 years. When Cyrus the Great comes to power he lets Israel return home. This Psalm comes with the Edict of Cyrus, when Israel had not yet been released, but would experience restoration soon.

Theologians call this the "Already – Not Yet" condition. The Christian experiences this condition in many ways. We have this new life in Christ, yet we struggle with the last vestiges of sin until restoration in heaven. We already know that God is with us through difficulty, but we have not yet experienced the resolution, and still suffer the pain. The hope in living an Already –Not Yet life is in "his bag of seed." The seeds in the Christians bag are faith, hope and love, and this is what we must sow, even in times that bring tears. In due time those seeds will bring to our lives a harvest of joy!

Hebrews 10: 23, 24, 25

"Let us hold fast the confession of our hope without wavering, for He who promised is faithful;

And let us consider how to stimulate one another to love and good deeds,

Not forsaking our own assembling together, as is the habit of some, but encouraging one another, and all the more as you see the day drawing near."

Prayer

Help us to remember Lord what it means to be a part of the body of Christ. We are each of us called to be a source of unity for the congregation and the church. A church cannot run on two or three talented people. We are all responsible to love and encourage one other, to study and to share biblical truths , and to serve God and others using our spiritual gifts. Thank you for investing in us Lord, and help us to embrace every opportunity to use our abilities to bring glory to You.

Lent Devotional Twenty Ninth Day

According to a recent poll by Pew Research, 83% of Americans identify as Christians, but only 39% attend church. There are many reasons for this gap between a confession of faith and assembling together. And the reasons may range from dysfunctional churches to the many things to do on a week-end. There is also a new idea spreading over the religious landscape of being "spiritual" without the need for organized churches.

However, Hebrews teaches us that our faith cannot be separated from being a part of the Church. In fact, it should become even more important to us, as time moves closer to the return of Christ. It is where we encounter the faithfulness of God, receive encouragement to live in Christ, and support others to do the same. The Church is vital to our faith because it is the place where we learn to "hold fast the confession of our hope without wavering."

Take the time today to think about your church attendance. As Easter draws near, find a church to consistently attend, or recommit to the one you have.

I John 2: 25, 26, 27

"This is the promise which He Himself made to us: eternal life.

These things I have written to you concerning those who are trying to deceive you.

As for you, the anointing which you received from Him abides in you, and you have no need for anyone to teach you; but as His anointing teaches you about all things, and is true and is not a lie, and just as it has taught you, you abide in Him."

Prayer

Thank you Father for filling us with the power of the Holy Spirit. Your Spirit is the living force within us, patiently and faithfully carrying out the essential work needed to transform us. The Holy Spirit prays for us, reminds us of the words of Jesus, and lets us know that we are loved. In times of hardship and challenge He fortifies us with confidence, right thinking, and boldness in our speech. It is the Holy Spirit that confirms Your presence.

Lent Devotional Thirtieth Day

With the exception of the Pentecostals, the Holy Spirit usually doesn't get top billing in the Church. One of the reasons may be that the Bible often speaks of the Spirit in less concrete ways which can be hard to grasp for those who are less metaphysical in their thinking. With the Spirit's work often imperceptible to a person's senses, and with analogies like a dove, fire, living water, and even a "Ghost," it may be a bit tough to relate to this member of the Trinity.

The Apostle John gives us another analogy; an anointing of God. I think we can grasp this one if we think of Christ, and then relate it to the Holy Spirit. Jesus has the title "Messiah," which means "The Anointed One." To anoint someone is to set them apart for a special reason. Jesus, as the Son of God, was set apart to minister, teach, and be a sacrifice. Jesus sent the Holy Spirit, to set us apart, to be like Him. This means the Spirit provides everything we need to follow Christ. This is the anointing that we have received from Christ, which also gives us the ability to distinguish a lie from truth.

Habakkuk 2: 9, 10, 11

"Woe to him who gets evil gain for his
   house
To put his nest on high,
To be delivered from the hand of
   Calamity!

You have devised a shameful thing
   For your house
By cutting off many peoples;
So you are sinning against yourself.

Surely the stone will cry out from the
   Wall,
And the rafter will answer it from the
   Framework."

Prayer

We pray Father to always bring glory to You in the way we live our lives. We desire to bear good fruit in our relationships, our work, and our service to You and others. We ask that You bring people into our lives who exhibit the same honesty, humility, and personal integrity that we value and strive for in all we do.

Lent Devotional Thirty First Day

In Luke 7:35 Jesus quotes a wisdom saying, "Wisdom is known by her children." This was an answer to his critics who were trying to prove that he was not the Messiah. Essentially, Jesus was telling them to look at the results of his work. They would prove if he were the Messiah or not.

Habakkuk was speaking about the witness of the Babylonians' true character. They prided themselves on what they had achieved in their various conquests of other nations, in disobedience and defiance of God. The results of their plunder, the homes they built, testified not to their glory, but to the fact that it had been achieved through "evil gain."

When Jesus entered Jerusalem and the crowds were praising him as the new King, the authorities tried to quiet them. But Jesus said "if these become silent the stones would cry out."

How a person lives their life, says volumes about their true character. What are the results of our work? If the walls and rafters of our homes could cry out, what would they say about us?

Isaiah 53: 12

"Therefore, I will allot Him a portion
  With the great,
And He will divide the booty with the
  Strong;
Because He poured out Himself to
  Death,
And was numbered with the
  transgressors;
Yet He Himself bore the sin of many,
And interceded for the transgressors."

Prayer

Lord, You gave us the greatest gift in Your Son Jesus. Let us never take for granted the truth of His life and death. Help us reserve a quiet moment of every day to meditate on the beauty of His words, the hope in His promises, and the eternal future He sealed for us by His blood and resurrection. Help us to remember with wonder, gratitude and humility His ministry and sacrifice. We pray to always acknowledge and understand the profound blessing we have in a personal Savior.

Lent Devotional Thirty Second Day

Jesus quoted this passage from Isaiah, some six hundred years after it was written, at the conclusion of the Last Supper. It would have been well known to the disciples, as it was part of the messianic passages of Isaiah, which depict the Messiah as the Suffering Servant. However, the disciples were so emotionally wrapped up in the moment, hearing that Jesus would soon be arrested on criminal charges, they missed the connection.

And yet, right before them, the servant Jesus in obedience to God was willing to suffer and pour out his life unto death, becoming the only intercession between God and Humankind. The most amazing moment in the history of humanity was taking place and the disciples missed its significance.

Well, sometimes familiarity with a story, leads to no longer really grasping it. Are we so familiar with Jesus that we miss His significance? Are we so busy that we lose our sense of amazement? Today let's pause and think about what the Lord has done and give thanks to our Savior!

Isaiah 54: 9, 10

"For this is like the days of Noah to Me,
When I swore that the waters of Noah
Would not flood the earth again;
So I have sworn that I will not be
   Angry with you
Nor will I rebuke you.

For the mountains may be removed
   And the hills may shake,
But My lovingkindness will not be
   Removed from you,
And My covenant of peace will not
   Be shaken,
Says the Lord who has compassion
   on you."

Prayer

How blessed are we that Your great love is unchanging! It is the same yesterday, today, and forever! Only through Christ could we be made worthy of Your love. Only by Your grace, compassion, and goodness can we rise above a sinful world. You alone make it possible for the undeserving to be redeemed and the faithful to be saved

Lent Devotional Thirty Third Day

The French novelist, Jean-Baptiste Alphonse Karr, coined the phrase, "the more things change, the more they stay the same." I thought of this phrase when I read this passage of Isaiah, "For this is like the days of Noah to Me."

In each era of time from Noah to Isaiah to Paul, all the way to the present day, people are still doing what is right in their own eyes. People are as sinful as they have ever been, it only takes a perusal of our many media venues to see the truth of these statements.

However, something has changed. The broken relationship between us and God has been restored through Jesus the Christ! Sin is as present in the world as it has ever been, but now the righteousness of God has come. Through God's compassion for people, they can know his lovingkindness, and have a Covenant of Peace with Him.

As Bob Dillon sings, "times they are a changing." Let's make a point to share this change, this new covenant with God, with those God brings into our lives every day.

Psalm 31: 13, 14, 15a

"For I have heard the slander of
   many,
 Terror is on every side;
While they took counsel together
   Against me,
They schemed to take away my life.

But as for me, I trust in You, O Lord,
I say, 'You are my God."

My times are in your hand."

Prayer

 Heavenly Father, thank you for the peace and reassurance of Your love and Your Word. You will never leave the faithful, no matter the circumstance; no matter the sin. We are grateful that You will see us through our trials and restore us to joy. As Jesus turned first to prayer to focus His mind and heart, so should we. We pray to be forgiven for our transgressions and wrong thinking. We pray for Your hand on our lives and to be reconciled to You. We pray that our faith will always be greater than our fear.

Lent Devotional Thirty Fourth Day

The world can be a terrifying place. And because it can be, it seems I often think the worst. As a parent, there are all kinds of things that I worry about, particularly when my kids are gone somewhere without me.

It's easy to imagine something bad happening. But when I catch myself imagining the worst, I think, why should I focus my mind on the terrifying scenarios? I consciously work at replacing the scenarios that seem to naturally run through my mind with something positive. I think this is what the Psalmist was doing. I commit the words of the Psalmist to my mind. A continuous prayer, almost a mantra that conditions the mind to follow my faith.

You can do the same. It's been proven, you can change the pattern of your mind. When things seem to overwhelm you, or the worst scenarios keep playing through your head, reach out to God with this positive prayer, "I trust in You, O Lord, I say, 'You are my God. My times are in your hand.'"

Luke 19: 32, 33, 34

"So those who were sent went away and found it just as He had told them.

As they were untying the colt, its owners said to them, 'Why are you untying the colt?'

They said, 'The Lord has need of it."

Prayer

Thank you Lord that each one of us matters to You and each one of us plays an important role in furthering Your Kingdom. No matter how small or how great, we have the opportunity to use our abilities to bring glory to Your name. How wonderful that You do not compare us! You do not judge us on our abilities, You only judge us on what we do with them! We pray to be aware of the ways in which we might please You and bring You praise. Give us the heart of a humble servant, especially when our sinful nature resists. Lord, we pray to be ready, willing, and able to respond to Your requests at any given time.

Lent Devotional Thirty Fifth Day

One of the most mysterious and wonderful ways of God is that He works out his purpose in the world through ordinary people and the resources they have available.

When Jesus was going to Jerusalem for his final week, he sent two of his disciples to a village which was on the way to Jerusalem. He told them to retrieve a young donkey, which they would find tied to a post. If anyone asks them why they were taking it, they were to reply, "The Lord has need of it." Sure enough, when they came to the village they saw the donkey, and the owner asked them why they were taking it. They replied as Jesus had instructed them, and apparently, the owner let it go because later that day the donkey was used in the Triumphal Entry.

The mystery is "who was that owner?" I have so many questions. But no answer is given, only a wonderful example of someone who is willing to give what the Lord needs. During Lent, let us rededicate ourselves to following the owner's example, and willingly give what the Lord needs.

Philippians 2: 5, 6, 7, 10, 11

"Have this attitude in yourselves which was also in Christ Jesus,

Who although He existed in the form of God, did not regard equality with God a thing to be grasped,

But emptied Himself, taking the form of a bond-servant, and being made in the likeness of men.

...so that at the name of Jesus every knee will bow, of those who are in heaven and on earth and under the earth,

And that every tongue will confess that Jesus Christ is Lord, to the glory of God the father."

Prayer

We pray to be worthy of the mission You have entrusted us with, Father. You have chosen us to represent the love and message of Christ and share it throughout the world. Help us to keep our eyes on the things above and our feet on the path that glorifies Your name.

Lent Devotional Thirty Sixth Day

This is the amazing, mysterious, wonderful story that Christians celebrate in their faith; The Infinite God takes finite form. He lives among finite beings and gives them the opportunity to experience the infinite with God.

Although God didn't have to do this, He choose to, and "emptied Himself" into a frail humanity bound by space and time. Of course, this all happened in Jesus Christ, whose attitude in the process was one of a servant.

If we believe in this story, we must have this same attitude of servanthood in ourselves. Servanthood is the way we must reach out to others with the story of salvation. We must empty ourselves into the lives of others, so that they might come to know and confess that Jesus is Lord.

Lent is the season we give something up to take on something new. Our lives are often so busy that we have "no time for anyone else." What must we give up, that will make room in our lives, to be a servant for Christ?

John 12:10, 11

"But the chief priests planned to put Lazarus to death also;

Because on account of him many of the Jews were going away and were believing in Jesus."

Prayer

Lord, we see Your sovereign power over life and death in the resurrection of Jesus. We behold Your authority in the created order of life and know that You are both our origin and our destiny. Our salvation is of the Lord and from the Lord and our assurance of eternal life is validated in the miracle of the resurrected Christ. We worship and praise You for Your forgiveness and compassion! We are blessed by a love that transcends our humanity and are redeemed by an undeserving grace that would have us live in the presence of a Holy God. It is both deeply humbling and profoundly empowering to be a witness for the resurrected Christ and a testimony to His sacrifice. May we always be faithful to the truth.

Lent Devotional Thirty Seventh Day

The fact that Lazarus had died and Jesus had resurrected him from the dead, was the heart of Lazarus' testimony. It placed him in a precarious position. Between the new kingdom of Christ and the old realm of the Chief Priest.

He was living proof of Jesus' miraculous power and many people were beginning to follow Jesus on account of his testimony. His life was undeniable evidence to Jesus' claim of Messiahship. On the other hand, it drew people away from the religious leaders, some of whom were teaching that there was no resurrection from the dead. This caused a conflict between him and the old world, even to the point that they were scheming to kill him.

We may not realize it but we are in the same spot. We have been "resurrected" from spiritual death to new life. When our lives are evidence of Jesus' power many will come to know him. But we must always be aware that some will try to silence our witness. When this happens, never forget, that our lives are the undeniable evidence and living proof of the Savior's power.

I Corinthians 1: 27

"But God has chosen the foolish things of the world to shame the wise, and God has chosen the weak things of the world to shame the things which are strong."

Prayer

Father, thank you for the strength of position You give us with Your love. We come to You in humility, confessing our transgressions and our shame, asking for forgiveness and praying for reconciliation. The world may see this as weakness, but we know the power and courage that comes from obedience and submission to Your plan for our lives. Peace and confidence come from Your Word. Hope is possible because of Your promise of a New Earth. Joy is ours because You fulfill our profound need to be loved. Grace is ours as the Holy Spirit transforms our thoughts, clarifies our purpose, and gives new meaning to everything we say and do. Thank you for the supernatural strength that is ours alone in Jesus Christ.

Lent Devotional Thirty Eighth Day

Most people enjoy the story about an underdog that wins, or the weak character who perseveres to overcome the stronger one. When we read the Bible we come across many examples of this formula, the most famous of which is David and Goliath. This is such a predominant theme in the Bible because it is a revelation of God's nature.

Our society often negates this Christian teaching as archaic and foolish. No surprise because within the social arena of ideas, Christian thought is regularly viewed as passé and weak. What our society propagates as the best relationships, truest ethic, and wisest course of action is frequently outside of God's design.

The Apostle Paul tells us what may look to the world as archaic, foolish, passé, and weak is actually the strongest position. One that can strip away society's facade of righteousness and expose its foolishness and sin. It is a baby born in a manger, itinerate teacher on a dusty road, a forsaken criminal on a cross. It all looked weak, until Easter morning!

Hebrews 12: 1, 2, 3

"Therefore, since we have so great a cloud of witnesses surrounding us, let us also lay aside every encumbrance and the sin which so easily entangles us, and let us run with endurance the race that is set before us.

Fixing our eyes on Jesus, the author and perfecter of faith, who for the joy set before Him endured the cross, despising the shame, and has set down at the right hand of the throne of God.

For consider Him who has endured such hostility by sinners against Himself, so that you will not grow weary and lose heart."

Prayer

Thank you Lord for giving wonderful examples of men and women in the Bible who were steadfast in their faith. They studied, they prayed, and they taught without ceasing. They endured hardships, dangers of persecution and sacrificed unto death to proclaim Your truth. They were long-suffering and patient. We pray to have their discipline and devotion.

Lent Devotional Thirty Ninth Day

"For every finish-line tape a runner breaks -- complete with the cheers of the crowd and the clicking of hundreds of cameras -- there are the hours of hard and often lonely work that rarely gets talked about." This quote from running legend, the late Grete Waitz, who was the 9-time winner of the New York City Marathon, helps us capture the essence of our passage in Hebrews.

The word "endurance" is a pretty important word in the Christian life. It means sticking to the "hours of hard and often lonely work" laying "aside every encumbrance and the sin which so easily entangles us." Grete did not become a 9-time marathon winner by being entangle in a sedentary lifestyle. She endured her daily workouts keeping her eyes on the prize.

Like Grete, we must "run with endurance the race that is set before us." Enduring to daily perfect our faith by "fixing our eyes on Jesus," who has won the race, and gives us the strength through the Holy Spirit to do the same. So today do not grow weary or lose heart. Run the race!

Matthew 3: 2, 3, 11b, 12

"Repent, for the kingdom of heaven is at hand.

For this is the one referred to by Isaiah the prophet when he said,
   'The voice of one crying in the
      wilderness,
   Make ready the way of the Lord,
   Make His paths straight!'

…He will baptize you with the Holy Spirit and fire.

His winnowing fork is in His hand, and He will thoroughly clear His threshing floor; and He will gather His wheat into the barn, but He will burn up the chaff with unquenchable fire."

Prayer

Jesus, we anticipate Your coming with great joy! Until such time, we will rededicate our lives to You daily. We will sing praises and glorify Your precious name! We will worship You in fear and awe until You return for us.

Lent Devotional Fortieth Day

In the mid-west, where I grew up, it wasn't unusual to have winter storms the first weeks of March but milder weather by the end of the month. It would often be said that March, "came in like a lion and left like a lamb." We could almost turn this saying around when it comes to the Lord Jesus. His first appearance was like a lamb, but his second will be like a lion. We don't know when He will come, but we do know His return will be powerful. It will be as the military says, "shock and awe!"

And when Jesus comes, as John the Baptist prophesied, He will set up His Kingdom on earth and judge the quick and the dead.

In many ways the times in which we live are like one big season of Lent, each day coming closer to Christ's return. So what do we do until that day of shock and awe arrives? We take the baptism of the Holy Spirit and the fire that it gives us in our souls to be "the voice of one crying in the wilderness, make ready the way of the Lord, make His paths straight!"

Prayer for Sunday

Father we thank you for the privilege of coming to You in prayer. We desire to strengthen our relationship with You and reconcile our sin with Your loving forgiveness. We sin against Your will and we sin against Your commandments. Even in our best actions we sin. We cannot rise above our humanity without Your grace.

We pray for those who love You and especially for those who do not know You. In this season, we ask that You reveal Your goodness and mercy to loved ones yet lost to us in this lifetime. We pray for a divine intervention on the hardened hearts of those who would deny You as our savior and redeemer.

Bless us with gifts of boldness and wisdom as we share the message of good news with others. May the words we speak reflect accurately the story of Your death and resurrection and the gift of eternal salvation that is available to all who would believe.

Help us to be examples of what holy transformation should look like in the world. Smooth our rough edges and soften our tones. Help us to speak Your Word with humility, gentleness, and clarity. We desire to please You and bring glory to Your holy name.

Prayer for Sunday

Heavenly Father, we desire a rich prayer life. It may not come naturally to us so we are thankful for the presence of the Holy Spirit who reminds us to pray first in all things. It is a relief and a comfort to know that You truly listen to our confessions and encourage us to lay all of our burdens before You in prayer. We expose the darkest parts of who we are and yet You forgive us and restore us to hope. We cry out in despair and You hold out Your hand to lift us up.

We reveal our shame and You make us clean again. We are deeply humbled to learn that nothing we do can separate us from Your love. In Your infinite goodness You would cherish us even though we grieve Your heart.

Forgive our foolishness and rebellion.
Forgive us for hurting those around us and for promoting ourselves above others.

We know that You hate sin and You hate for us to be in sin. Please steer us away from evil and away from those who would bring destruction upon us. We pray to be able to discern Your will for our lives and embrace the blueprint You have uniquely designed for us.

Prayer for Sunday

Father, it is hard to know how to begin to express our appreciation and gratitude for the blessings You have bestowed upon us as believers. The ministry of Jesus changed the world and His death and resurrection turned it upside-down. You are the creator and sustainer of life, and yet when we first turned from You and toward sin You did not abandon us. You saved us from our wretched selves with the sacrifice of Your beloved Son, Jesus. With this act, You defined true love: True love is selfless, immeasurable, forgiving, and sacrificial. We may fail You, Lord, but Your love never fails us.

We thank You for blessings undeserved and for blessings unexpected. When we walk with You we secure for ourselves peace, confidence, and hope. We are rewarded for our obedience with grace and favor. When we trust in Your will for our lives, we can live without fear and apprehension. When we accept the gift of salvation we can rest in the knowledge that we will live in Your presence forever. Your great love salvages lives that are fraught with suffering and despair and inspires the human heart to press on through hardship.

Prayer for Sunday

Thank you for revealing Yourself to us through Jesus. We desire to pour out our hearts in gratitude for Your Word, Your Son, and Your everlasting love. Although we can never escape our human nature, we want to live moral and honest lives and be accountable to You for the choices we make. We thank you for the Holy Spirit who makes it possible for us to grow and mature in our Christian walk.

Thank you for being the Father we can always depend on for support and encouragement. We pray to accept Your discipline in humility and make the changes that we know will ultimately prosper us and those we love. Help us to be flexible in our thinking so that we might embrace corrections with ease and understanding rather than struggle with our nature to resist. Thank you for Your patience with us as we understand more and more what it means to submit and to be obedient to Your Word.

We honor You Lord, in prayer and in worship. We honor You as individual believers and as the collective body of Christ. We listen to music and read Scripture and in some special part of our hearts we are touched, thank you for those beautiful moments of fellowship with You.

Prayer for Sunday

"It is good to sing praises to our God; for it is pleasant and praise is beautiful." Psalm 147

We are thankful Father, to be part of a spiritual family that is committed to You. We are bound to each other by our devotion and obedience to You. It is a privilege that we honor and a responsibility that we accept. We pray that the Holy Spirit will help us use our gifts in worthy and sincere service to You and others. By this we hope that others will see a reflection of Your love in us. We praise You with our whole hearts and thank you for the opportunity to change the world.

Thank you for raising up godly leaders in the church who model personal obedience and teach us by example. They nourish us with Your truth and shepherd us with Your care and concern. We are blessed by those whose are gifts are evangelical or pastoral. However, we are always mindful that it is Your power that allows any of us to speak out for Jesus and witness for Him. You alone deserve the glory for the work that is in us.

Our love for You takes up residence in our hearts like a song whose melody we like to hum.

ABOUT THE AUTHORS

The devotions were written by John M. Scholte. John is a Professor of Religion and Humanities and C.E.O. of Scholte Consulting Services. He is also a Minister in the Reformed Church in America. John lives in San Diego, California, with his wife and five children.

The prayers were written by Germaine Griffiths. Germaine lives in San Diego, CA. She is an award winning special educator retired from the Encinitas Union School District. Germaine is currently attending Calvary Chapel Bible College in Murrieta, CA.

For more educational resources see Scholte Consulting Services website at:

www.scholteconsulting.com

Waiting for the Forty First Day!

Copyright ©2016 by Scholte Consulting Services

Published by CreateSpace Independent Publishing Platform (January 2016)

Scholte Consulting Services
13223-1 Black Mountain Rd #377
San Diego, CA 92126

Scriptures taken from the NEW AMERICAN STANDARD BIBLE®, Copy © 1960, 1962, 1968, 1971, 1972, 1973, 1975, 1977, 1995 by The Lockman Foundation. Used by permission.

Cover Photo: ©David Monsma/Scholte Consulting Services

All rights reserved.

Printed in the United States of America.

The authors wish to thank Ronald Scholte for his assistance in editorial review of the manuscript.

www.scholteconsulting.com

Made in the USA
Middletown, DE
14 February 2017